TRASH AND TREASURE

DISCLAIMER

This book contains information gathered primarily through experience and is as factual and accurate as the authors have been able to make it. The suggestions given are not intended to be legal advice and should not be considered as such.

TRASH and TREASURE

The Complete Book About Garage Sales

by
Jack and Chris Wilkie

Bent Twig

TRASH AND TREASURE
The Complete Book About Garage Sales

Published by: **Bent Twig Publishing Co.**
1088 Irvine, Blvd., Suite 329
Tustin, California 92680

Cover Illustration by Joel Barbee

All rights reserved. No part of this book may be reproduced or transmitted in any form or by any means, electronic or mechanical, including photocopying, recording or by any information storage and retrieval system without written permission from the authors, except for the inclusion of brief quotations in a review.

Copyright © 1987 by Jack and Chris Wilkie
First Printing 1988
Printed in the United States of America

Library of Congress Catalog Card Number: 87-73354

ISBN 0-945221-00-2

FOREWARD

When the chronicles of the last quarter of the Twentieth Century are written, historians may record the existence of a strange phenomenon.

It came about primarily because of an overabundance of material goods in an affluent society . . . and the fact that some members of that society were reluctant to discard items that were still serviceable. Instead they sold them. From this a quasi industry evolved.

But that's not the phenomenon.

It's the subculture that evolved with the quasi industry; made up of people who would spend most of their free time going to sales when they didn't need anything to buy things they would never use—and who curiously found pleasure in the whole experience.

ACKNOWLEDGEMENTS

Thanks to these friends, associates, competitors and others whom we see regularly or irregularly on our weekend rounds.
The Dresser Man and His Wife
Marcy
Ichabod Crane
Walter
The Pushy One
Little Joyce and Her Mother
The Jewelry Lady with the Slipping Teeth
My Friend Jerry
The Guy Who Collects World War II Souveniers
The Man in the Station Wagon Who Keeps
    His Motor Running
The Tall Pretty Gray Haired Lady Who Should Be Home
    Cooking For Her Husband
The Mexican Family in the Van

And special thanks for their help in putting this book together:
Julie Myhra
Arley Cristianson
Chuck and Nancy Cook
Roger Wilkie

TABLE OF CONTENTS

I WHY HAVE A GARAGE SALE?   17
    There are many reasons, all of them valid; but a garage sale isn't the answer for selling everything

II PLANNING YOUR OWN GARAGE SALE   21
    • What do you have to sell? • Scheduling • Block or Neighborhood Sales • Hitchhiking

III PROMOTION   27
    • Advertising Methods • What Your Ad Should Say • Guard Your House • Placing the Ad • Radio and Television • Signs Add a Distinctive Touch • Trail Blazing • Watch Your Arrow Points • Putting Up the Signs • Take Them Down

IV PREPARING FOR THE SALE   43
    • Is It Worth It? • How Do You Display Merchandise? • Garage Doors Can Be Trouble • Other Clothes Racks • Tables As Counters • Ground Level Display • Price Everything • Plan Your Attack • Security • Setting Up • The Luxury of Time • A Faster Pace • Getting Your Business Straight • "Let's Have A Sale Together!" • Don't Forget Change • Last...But Foremost: Safety!

V THE SALE   63
    • The All-Important Cashbox • Opening Up • Kids • Other Points • Taking Deposits • Should You Take Checks? • So Much For Fame • Keep It Moving • Explain This One

VI YOU BE THE CUSTOMER   77
    • How's Your Attitude? • How About Clothes? • Getting Started • The Big Day • Negotiating: My Price Or Yours? • The Bud Vase • What Do You Say? • Caveat Emptor? • By the Way

VII FIRMLY COMMITTED...OR, WHO CARES?   93

Introduction

SATURDAY MORNING MADNESS

"Garage sales aren't anything new," the man said as he looked over a card table full of knicknacks. "They aren't any different from the flea markets of North Africa or the weekend bazaars you find in Europe."

"Yes," a second man said. "I went to one in Rome. They have it every Sunday in a lane near the Porte Portese. An interesting place."

Wonderful. It was ten o'clock on a Saturday morning in June, and we had a backyard full of globetrotting philosophers. We have always preferred big spenders.

"There's a big difference," another man chimed in. "In those places, the sellers are professionals, or at least semiprofessionals. They sell merchandise to the public all the time, not just once a year or so. So they're merchants. That's the difference."

The first man's wife had left the book table and moved over to join the conversation. "How about rummage sales? Churches have been holding them as long as--well, since my grandmother's time, anyway."

"Right." Her husband confirmed it. "That's all a garage sale really is--a rummage sale. The only difference is, instead of taking your stuff to a central point like a church or clubhouse to sell it--and remember, the sellers are all amateurs-you hold your own sale at home."

Each speaker obviously had his point. But the fact is, the garage sale, or yard sale, is a genuinely unique American function. (Since we've been to garage sales in Canada, we include Canadians. After all, they're Americans too.) In some places the garage sale is so well established that it can now be called an American institution. And while people have been selling their unwanted possessions to other people for hundreds of years, what has evolved in this country is unlike all that went before...as you'll learn in this book.

This is a how-to and how-not-to book. It tells you how to have your own garage or yard sale and how to get the most out of going to other people's. It also has tips that will help you avoid mistakes whether you're on the selling or the buying end.

People everywhere are doing both. Some do it for profit, but most do it for fun. They laugh and say they're buying and selling other people's junk. "One man's junk is another man's treasure" is repeated Saturday after Saturday in every corner of North America. The authors know this firsthand, having been involved with garage and rummage sales in cities and towns from one end of this continent to another. And they've found more similarities than differences.

In Southern California, garage saling has been refined to a science. What began for some as a hobby has been transformed into a profitable full-time business. Others never care whether what they're doing pays or not--they're having more fun than ever.

Lasting friendships have been formed among garage salers. Despite age differences, economic or ethnic backgrounds, the Garage Sale Junkies have formed a loose band of friends. They greet each other warmly when they meet at the first stop of the day. Some Saturdays they'll meet several times along their routes; then not see each other for several weeks when their paths don't cross.

They're not above a bit of competitive one-upmanship, such as brandishing a sterling silver whatnot and proclaiming, "Look what I found in the 50c junkbox over at that sale on First Street! Oh, you haven't been there yet? Too bad. The prices were really low. I suppose everything's pretty well picked over by now."

They learn each other's first names and seldom their last names. But they get to know each other well enough to remember each other's likes and dislikes...what they're looking for in particular. Some even exchange gifts. After meeting on someone's lawn, a woman will say to another, "Oh, I just remembered. I have something in my trunk for you!" And a figurine or a mystery novel or some missing piece to a collection will be brought out and presented. Later in the year, the item may be giftwrapped and presented as a Christmas present--to someone known only as Sally --or who is remembered only as "The Girl Who Collects Old Crockery."

There are different reasons for having a sale. Charity, the noblest, is usually behind an organization's annual event. Get-

---

"If you can't make money at a garage sale, you probably can't make money at anything."
-Horace Greeley

ting rid of the accumulation of years to lighten the moving load is a sound reason. Or even if one's not moving. Some people set up everything they own in the garage area behind their apartment, hoping they'll raise enough money to pay the rent. Or have a party. Whatever.

Garage sales can be organized to the point of irritation, or they can be totally chaotic, which is equally irritating. Most fall somewhere in between. Visiting garage sales as a customer also has its rewards and pitfalls. The purpose of this book is to show you how to do both better, with as much or as little effort as you're willing to expend. The results will be proportional.

We try not to be preachy, just factual...sometimes rather loosely. We also hope you'll find some of the sidelights and stories entertaining.

Some information may seem elementary. It's given to make sure that everything's covered for those just starting out. And if some of the do-and-don't tips make you feel that we're insulting your intelligence, remember that we've seen and experienced incidents at garage sales that prompted them. More than once. We'll always marvel at the dumb and thoughtless things that supposedly intelligent suburban residents can do.

So whether you're a rookie or an old pro, have fun garage saling. Good luck. And we hope you find the Buy of the Century!

Chapter I

WHY HAVE A GARAGE SALE?

Silly question.

There are a dozen reasons. If the attic or garage or the basement or all three are so crammed with junk that you can't move .... gather it up, stick on some prices, and sell ... it all!

What's a better reason than moving? If you're aware that moving companies charge by weight as well as mileage, you know that the more you can reduce the weight of your shipment, the less the move will cost you. So look around the house for heavy items that you can live without. Being able to live without them is important--especially when your baleful eye lands on your books and records.

There's no problem if you're a casual collector. The more books and albums you can part with, the lower your moving bill. But more serious collectors, beware. Look elsewhere for things to jettison ... because you may have regrets later. Can you go the rest of your life without ever hearing "Pine Top's Boogie Woogie?"

The best thing is to have a "moving" sale before you call movers for estimates. That way you have eliminated the not-needed stuff and saved the goodies. One family's experience shows what can happen.

When preparing to move cross-continent, the Taylors were so shocked at the high estimates from the movers that they decided the only thing to do was "get rid of everything."

It was said half-seriously, but somehow the thought became stuck in their minds.

Their sale was a beauty.

They sold many inexpensive items that could be replaced quickly at their destination. That made sense. But then as the sale progressed, something happened. That serious concern they had for keeping moving cost low turned into panic--and the compulsion to sell literally everything in sight.

Like sharks at a feeding frenzy, they grabbed for more things to sell. No longer thinking rationally, they sold Dad's favorite chair, Mom's collection of cookbooks, the record albums--things they'd never replace.

Needless to say, the Taylors reduced their moving bill to a fraction of what it was. And they had a pile of cash, too. But they didn't have the things they loved. Their family treasures were gone.

Because of their weight and bulk, appliances and pianos are the most expensive things to move. Look closely at yours and ask yourself if you couldn't use one just like it instead of the

---

> "It is better to sell an item at a price lower than you wanted than not to sell it--and have it staring at you all year long."
>
> -Desmond Fook

original. Then sell it. The money you make on the item, plus the money you save on your moving bill will in most cases be enough to replace it. And in some cases you may be able to upgrade to a newer or better model.

If your piano is a fine musical instrument, of course, it may be expensive to replace in your new city. But if it's just a good, serviceable upright, get some of your muscled friends to help you move it out to the driveway. You'll be surprised at how fast it will sell.

Other reasons for having garage sales include raising money for charity, or for the rent money, or to get together with some neighbors whom you've been trying to cultivate. Some people have garage sales every Saturday, trying to sell the same junk they had for sale the week before; hoping to make enough money to buy a sixpack and a bag of Fritos.

IS IT THE ANSWER FOR EVERYTHING?

A garage sale is not the place to sell great grandma's lapis beads, however, even if you know their value and are willing to sell them for half price or less. It's much better to put them in a consignment jewelry or antique shop and pay the commission. That way, you'll get the highest price, with no worries about them being stolen, or having to turn down low-ball offers. The same goes for mom's mink stole, that 1920 cherry secretary, or anything of real value. Consignment shops take anything from 15% to 50%, and if you're not happy with the deal offered you're always free to leave and find some other shop.

(As a buyer, though, valuable items at low prices are what you love to find!)

Chapter II

PLANNING YOUR OWN GARAGE SALE

The best way to prepare for your own garage sale is to learn what others do. Be a buyer before you become a seller. Visit other garage sales and observe.

Spend at least two or three weekends seeing how others do it. What are they doing wrong? Are there enough signs to lead you to the place? Is the merchandise arranged so it's easy to inspect? (Only an idiot tries to sell books out of a deep carton that prevents customers from reading the titles. But you see it all the time.) Is all the merchandise price-marked? Remember the prices and note how they compare with the same merchandise at other sales.

Be observant. As a customer you'll see items displayed poorly, hear the owners make statements that ruin sales, find different things that irritate you. Take it all in. Profit by their mistakes so that you can have a sale that will be better run, attended by more people, and make more money.

Don't stop at checking out garage sales. Visit thrift stores. Go to the Salvation Army and Goodwill stores to get ideas. Compare prices. Determine quality and condition. Remember, these people are old pros at pricing. If you want to be successful, your prices should be the same, if not lower.

WHAT DO YOU HAVE TO SELL?

Do you really have enough merchandise to hold a garage sale? You'll often see sales that amount to one card table full of knicknacks and a few broken toys lying on the driveway. These accomplish nothing except to give some bored housewives something to do on a Saturday. Many cars, attracted by the signs, will drive by slowly, take two or three seconds to assess the possibilities, then speed away because they see nothing of interest. Time is valuable to them. They won't waste it by leaving their cars for pure junk.

Big merchandise stops cars. If you have any furniture for sale, plan to put it out near the curb so they see it first.

Visibility is vital. Plan to hang up some streamers or banners, or even the American Flag. Attract attention. Slow down that traffic! Look festive!

SCHEDULING

How many days are you planning to be open? The big day is Saturday, of course. Customers can be attracted on Friday and Sunday, too, but usually in smaller numbers. Decide if it's worth it to be open on two or even three days, because remember, the sale will take your full time. Try to schedule your sale on a Saturday after the First or the Fifteenth of the month--

when people have had a payday and have money to spend.

The time of year is important, too. You certainly don't want to schedule your sale in the middle of the rainy season. Not just because your merchandise and signs will get wet, but also because few customers will venture out to shop on such days. Similarly, don't plan a sale on a day that conflicts with a big holiday or event. Take a close look at the calendar before you set the date.

Ask friends you can count on to help you with the sale. Garage sales take work and time. Line up your manpower well in advance.

"Watch it. She had those same cookies at her sale six months ago. I mean, those same cookies."

BLOCK OR NEIGHBORHOOD SALES

In neighborhoods where everyone is compatible, what's wrong with everyone having a sale at the same time? It doesn't take a great deal of organizing...merely some neighbor-to-neighbor phonecalls, or a flyer saying something like this...

LET'S EVERYBODY ON PATTON LANE HAVE A GARAGE SALE ON MARCH 19!

Gather up all your wonderful junk (and even some real goodies) and put it all out for sale in your driveway on Sat. March 19 starting at 8 a.m. If we all chip in on the ad in the Shopper, the individual cost will be peanuts. Also, if you want to help out making and putting up signs—or help in other ways,

CALL **CONNIE SMITH** **853-8769**

Not a bad idea, is it? Lots of homes pitching in means lots of merchandise to the garage sale customers, and they'll be there in droves. Especially if the neighbors go all out with the decorating.

HITCH HIKING

Some people are annoyed when a neighbor down the street, knowing that they're planning a garage sale, opens up with their own, hoping to cash in on the flow of customers in the neighborhood. If it were to happen time after time, with no attempt made to communicate between the households, and the original family was the only one putting up signs and placing ads--would it be cause for justifiable homicide? Not really. If it happens to you, try to get them to join in. If they won't, don't waste your time fretting about it. There will always be leeches in the world. Ignore them.

Even look on the bright side: two garage sales in a block are better than one.

Hard to believe, but this was at a sale in one of the nicer neighborhoods. The merchandise was set out in boxes for the customers to weed through. Needless to say, most of them took one look and went back to their cars.

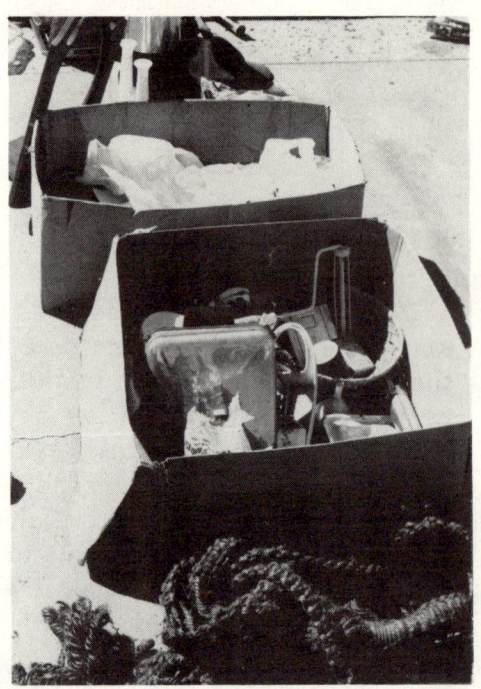

In another nice (no kidding!) neighborhood, this was the view as you approached the garage sale. Really makes you want to buy everything in sight, doesn't it?

Chapter III

PROMOTION

Someone once said, "Doing business without advertising is like winking at a girl in the dark: You know what you're doing, but nobody else does." Advertising is just as important for your garage or yard sale as it is for a billion-dollar corporation. It's based on a simple principle. The more attention you draw to your sale, the more traffic you generate, and the more sales you stand to make.

ADVERTISING METHODS

Display is the most basic form of advertising. Put the merchandise in the proper place to draw attention to itself (see Chapter IV). Unless, however, people happen to drive or walk down your street, they won't see your terrific display and won't know about the sale. That's why you put signs up on strategic corners. And why you make flyers (if you can have them copied cheaply enough) to stick under windshield wipers at the shopping center.

It would also be wonderful to take big ads in the newspapers and buy radio and television time. But they're obviously too expensive. You must keep costs down so that your sale makes a profit. Therefore you use affordable advertising media. The signs on strategic corners. Classified ads in the neighborhood shopper. And if it doesn't cost too much, perhaps a classified ad in the local newspaper.

In Southern California, the Pennysaver is the garage sale bible. It's the primary medium for advertising that must be purchased. (Signs you make are your primary advertising medium, but the costs involved should be minimal.) The Pennysaver is published in many different neighborhood editions which correspond to zipcodes. You have the flexibility to buy only the ones you need to reach your most likey prospects. You really can't expect to attract people more than five miles away, so don't bother advertising in more than your own and the adjacent zipcodes.

There is a shopper-type publication, sometimes more than one, in almost every community across the country. Chances are that no matter where you are, it's one of your most cost-effective media.

WHAT YOUR AD SHOULD SAY

To address all of the garage sale pros and amateur addicts, who never miss a word in the shopper, you don't have to be clever, simply clear. Tell them *what* (a garage sale), *when* (the dates, the days, and the times you open and close), *where* (your address), *and how to get there* (a cross street, a big intersection nearby, whatever it takes to make sure they can locate you). They will take it from there.

But there are others out there that won't be attracted by just the bare facts. They may be dilletantes; casual sale-goers who aren't fanatic about it. If you try something imaginative, you might catch their fancy. They probably won't be going to every sale advertised, but if you can give them something to think about, they'll be sure to visit yours.

Try an opening like, "Our front lawn is loaded!" Or, "Garage about to explode!" Or, "Neighborhood Sale of the Century!" Or, "Family heirlooms, giveaway prices!" For the collectors and for others who are looking for a specific item, add a few words about merchandise. Obviously you can't list everything. It isn't necessary. Certain words, however, will ring a bell with certain buyers. Such as antiques, lawn equipment, tools, appliances, jewelry, rare books, sporting goods. Include items that will bring you plenty of profit; eliminate the items that won't.

> WHAT A MOVING SALE! Everything goes - cheap! Toyota camper top, piano, furniture, etc. May 2&3, 8-4. 1768 Irving St. Anytown (Carver/Stahl)

Don't put your phone number in the ad. If you do, people will start calling you long before the sale and want to come to your house ahead of time. They're the merchants from used furniture stores and swap meets. Others will call and want to do their shopping over the phone...to save them a trip to your place. Don't encourage any of them. The truth is, even if you don't include the number in your ad, there will be some people who have access to special telephone directories that are listed by addresses. They'll provide all the annoyance you need.

We know of one woman who comes to the door the night before a sale and says that she can't come in the morning because of her grandmother's funeral--and can she please have a look at the things you'll be selling. At last count, her grandmother has been buried eight times.

You may not object to admitting someone into your garage or patio early, feeling that, after all, it's another chance to sell your merchandise. But the disadvantages outweight the advantages. Pre-sale shoppers are usually shrewd and often high pressure; they're not about to pay your marked prices, and many times will offer you a lump sum for an entire collection of articles. The result is a great loss of potential profit on the following day, and you stand the chance of opening your sale without one of the items that you listed in your advertisement.

There's nothing worse than going to what sounded like a fine sale and hearing, "Oh, someone came by last night and took most of what we had." You've wasted your time.

In the interest of fair play, it's best to set a firm policy: "No Pre-Sales." If you have experiences with "sooners" before, you may want to even state this in your ad. But you'll be giving everyone the same opportunity to see and buy what you have to sell. And you'll be giving yourself the optimum profit opportunity.

GUARD YOUR HOUSE

At the same time that you don't want to encourage pre-sale people, you don't want to invite thieves, either--especially if

> "I love collectors. If you have something they want, they'll pay you handsomely for it. But watch out for dealers. They'll make you think they're doing you a favor for buying your worthless item."
>
> -Clarence Newfacky

you've advertised valuables. So don't go out the night before and leave your house unguarded!

PLACING THE AD

A great source of frustration is to open the shopper or the local paper to find that your advertisement has mistakes in it. Many times you have no one but yourself to blame. When you call to place the ad, have it already written out (this may sound elementary, but some people have been known to "wing it" and dictate to the ad taker as they go!) Read the copy slowly, speak clearly, and spell everything. Or, at least those words that might possibly be misunderstood. Be sure to add "avenue" or "street," "court," or whatever your street is designated.* Then --make sure that the ad taker reads every word back to you- spelling out everything!

This in itself is no guarantee that everything will go smoothly. The order takers at the publications, being human, make mistakes. Sometimes dreadful ones. The wrong date. The wrong address.

And, of course, once the issue appears, the damage is done.

We've known people who've screamed in rage at the paper- -only to be told by a voice over the telephone, "We're awfully sorry it happened. Would you like us to run a corrected version

---

This is especially important in certain areas. In South Florida, for instance, many cities have numbered street systems with NE, NW, SE and SW quadrants; and the designation of the street (street, avenue, court, etc.) tells whether it runs north-south or east-west. Unfortunately there's no standardization and the designations in Miami aren't the same as in Ft. Lauderdale, for instance. ❐ In Southern California, addresses are confusing in another way: the same town can have a Yucca St., Yucca Blvd., and a Yucca Circle, etc. Or, Yucca St. can be a "jumper" that runs for three blocks, stops, then picks up again several blocks away. Finding the particular section where a garage sale is being held can be murder, especially if you're from another neighborhood. So be sure to give the name of the cross street you're near and / or identify a prominent intersection nearby.

of the ad next week at no charge?"

Terrific.

Once in a while, in driving around-- following the day's list of garage sales--we'll stop at a home and find no sign of activity of any kind. Then we'll spot a note tacked to the front door: "Sorry, the Shopper goofed. Our garage sale was last week."

If your ad appears when you want it to . . . worded as you want it worded, spelled as you meant it to be spelled, rejoice!

"Oh, no! I forgot the automatic sprinklers!"

RADIO AND TELEVISION

While broadcast media may be out of reach for one family's garage sale, the airwaves are available to some others. If you have a legitimate organization that is holding a rummage sale, garage sale, church sale or whatever for charity, write to your local radio and tv stations and give them the facts.

They are required by government regulations to devote a certain amount of their airtime to public service announcements, and there's a good chance that your sale announcement can be included in their "Community Billboard" program.

SIGNS

Signs don't cost much and they can pull mightily. They should be big, simple and eyecatching, and they should be placed where lots of people will see them.

White cardboard is best. Colored board may catch the eye, but there will be less contrast between the lettering and the background and your sign may be harder to read. Brown corrugated carton sides will work, too, but make sure you use bright, contrasting colors for the lettering. White letters are fine. They're even better when they're outlined or given a black shadow. This takes time, but planning a garage sale should be a process extending over several weeks. Make your signs well in advance.

What seems to be a huge sign when you're lettering it at home will suddenly seem pitifully small when it's stapled to a telephone pole down at the corner. An 8-1/2" x 11" sign becomes a postage stamp. Almost invisible! A 2' x 3' sign is an attention-getter; even bigger ones attract even more.

It's not necessary to buy expensive Crescent Board at the art supply store. Keep your eyes open for big pieces of white cardboard all year long. Save them for making signs later--when you know a sale's coming up.

Don't be ashamed if you're not a great signpainter. Letter as neatly and clearly as you can, using big letters, and make them stand out. Remember this sign?

PLAN AHEAD

Avoid making this mistake by using a pencil and plotting where the letters will go before you actually start painting them or using markers. Chances are your pencil lines won't be seen from far away--so you won't even have to bother erasing them.

The two things to strive for--and this goes for any kind of advertising--are visibility and clarity. Ideally, yoursign should be fully legible from a moving car. Like the layout of your sign, keep the message simple. Do it like this, using three sizes of letters:

GARAGE SALE	(big)
SAT-SUN MAY 2-3	(medium)
1897 IRVING ST.	(big)
(NEAR CARVER)	(small)
TURN LEFT AT CHURCH	(small)

Leave the bottom line of the sign blank until you know where you're going to place it. Then, using small letters, you can add a specific instruction ("TURN LEFT AT CHURCH") or an arrow. You can make up a quantity of signs with arrows (shafts and no points) and add points on the arrows at the installation site.

Now that you've covered the essentials on your sign, do something to make them different from all the others. Give them all the same "look," a colored border or some symbol or device that people will recognize. Something that will convince those hundreds of people driving around neighborhoods that your sale is "a must." And if there are many, many garage sales that day-perhaps too many to cover in one day--yours is the one they won't want to miss. Because of something intriguing, creative or unique about your signs.

TRAIL BLAZING

You might try a simple 6-inch cartoon. Use a copy machine and make enough copies to paste one on every sign. Do it in color. Some people mark the route to their homes with simple arrows, placed in the middle of the block--just to show customers that they're on course. Do them one better. Use your symbol or cartoon along with arrows to give your signs some extra flair.

If you have no artistic talent and can't get someone to draw a cartoon for you, you might "borrow" one--on a very short, temporary basis, mind you--from a newspaper or magazine. You don't want detail; it must be a simple figure that can be recognized from a passing car. If your sale is mostly clothes, you might cut out a fashion shot of a model in a gown--if it has a plain white background. With sports equipment, a skier or a tennis player--or whatever's appropriate.

In the strictest sense, using someone else's artwork for a commercial purpose is illegal. But making a crude copy for a two-day garage sale sign will hardly inspire the artwork's owner to institute legal proceedings against you.

If all else fails, take a colored marker and create some kind of unique border around your signs--stars or symbols that are easy to draw and won't make the project too time-consuming. We recently saw signs with streamers of crepe paper stapled at the bottom. They added both color and motion as they swayed in the breeze. And they caught everyone's eye.

WATCH YOUR ARROW POINTS

The way arrows point on street and highway signs is unique. An arrow pointing straight up means "straight ahead," and an arrow pointing left or right means turn left or right at the next corner. For right and left turn signs, leave the points off the arrows until later.

PUTTING UP THE SIGNS

When it's time to put up signs, no one does a better job than Pete Dixon and his 12-year-old son, Bobby. They're up at six a.m., loading their station wagon with the signs, two hammers, a can of nails, silver duct tape, a roll of wire, a staple gun with extra staples, and string. That way, they're prepared for just about any affixing problem they may run into--tree trunk, telephone pole, stop sign, concrete light pole, fence, wall-you name it. They also pack a couple of black felt markers--to put the points on the arrows.

Pete and Bobby cover every direction away from the house, putting up at least one at a busy intersection. They go as far as six or eight blocks away. They look for obvious focal points; where people's eyes are likely to turn. They put up one or two at prominent points in shopping center parking lots. And when the Dixon family has a garage sale, people know it.

Not very artistic (and look at the way "foothill" is lettered), but it's really big and it does the job.

This kitchen table artistry looks fine, but couldn't they find bigger signboard?

This signmaker taped paper signs to the sides of a cardboard carton and placed it on a hedge out in front of the house. Keep your eyes open for other opportunities to attract attention.

There's a ditch at this street corner, so the guardrail makes a natural place to tape a box-sign.

TAKE THEM DOWN

This is important. Always remember where you put up the signs--so you can take them down--immediately after the sale. For three good reasons. 1) If they're left up, they'll be leading people to your house on the following weekend, long after your sale's over. 2) You may have a police officer show up at your door, your sign in one hand and a citation for littering in the other. 3) You may like having a garage sale (especially if it's successful) and want to have another. So save the signs. You can always paste a piece of paper over the date and letter in a new date.

"I know it's early, Jimmy, but we won't have time to put them up later."

Good idea: directional sign set on the roof of a car parked out front. The carton has rocks in it to keep it in place. A bigger carton would have been still better.

Pop Quiz: What is this sign instructing you to do?

Chapter IV

PREPARING FOR THE SALE

Like most projects, the more effort you are willing to put into your garage sale, the more rewarding it will be. The key is always attention to detail.

Make your merchandise as attractive as possible! Wash, repair, dust, polish, clean. Make your silver pieces gleam; your crystal and glassware shine. Then on sale day, put the silver in the sunlight--not in the back of the garage--so it will sparkle enticingly and be snapped up in a hurry.

> "Losing money on a garage sale is nature's way of telling you that you are a born loser."
>
> -Alfred E. Newman

IS IT WORTH IT?

The lazy person's attitude is, "Why bother? I'll sell it as is. Let them clean it." If that's the way you feel, fine. Sit back and relax and have another beer. But you might think about this: Compared to the thin dime that some dirty water glass you're selling might bring you, the price that one sparkling glass tumbler may bring could buy you a whole sixpack.

It's up to you to determine whether the effort is going to be worth it. You just judge how much more the item will bring when it's put in almost-new shape.

Think of it another way. A handyman is fortunate. He can buy things that don't work or are broken; take a little time fixing them--then sell them a week or so later at a fine profit. If he can do that with toys and appliances, wouldn't it be possible for you to do something similar--with silver or glassware, for instance? Your only investment would be in silver polish, detergent, time, and some elbow grease. If you kept at it, you could turn it into a profitable little sideline. Interested?

HOW DO YOU DISPLAY MERCHANDISE?

We already know that glassware and other shiny items belong in the sunlight. And big overstuffed furniture near the curb to attract attention from passing traffic. What about clothes and books? Skis and bicycles? Bowling balls and toasters? Appliances?

Wash clothes. Get the "old clothes" or closet smell out of them. Take them out of plastic bags when you display them. Don't dryclean things; it costs too much, and people ordinarily will have them drycleaned themselves after they purchase them. But brush all your nice garments and hang them neatly. Don't bother ironing, but smooth them out by hand. Do the same with sheets, pillowcases and tablecloths.

Sort them and display them according to the type of garment, then price them, either individually or with a sign signifying that everything on one rack is the same price. Each item should be hung on a clothes hanger. (You don't have to give the hanger to the customer when you sell something.) Don't hang the clothes so high that a five-foot woman can't get at them. Hang them on a clothes rack. If you know where to borrow one, do it. Try a charity organization. The Salvation Army and the Good Will Society seem to have changed their policy in some areas, but the St. Vincent de Paul Society will lend you the racks--if you donate the rest of your merchandise--the stuff that didn't sell--to them afterwards. This often works out well, because you're rid of a lot of items you don't want anymore; part of the mess is taken away instantly; and you end up with a tax deduction. (You are given a receipt, and you are usually allowed to state the value of the material you donated yourself.)

Simple clothes racks. Lengths of stout dowelling cut to fit between the porch posts are held up by closet pole holders and reinforced with wire in the middle.

GARAGE DOORS CAN BE TROUBLE

Unless they're propped up expertly, overhead garage doors aren't suitable for hanging clothes. They're not built to take the weight. Many of them have collapsed and a few people have been hurt. You could be on the receiving end of a dandy lawsuit if it happened in your driveway.

Even if there's no one under it at the time, when the door comes down, you're going to have a mess of dirty clothes on your hands. Let's hope you've swept your driveway thoroughly. That way, they won't be too dirty.

There are rental outfits that have clothes racks, but unfortunately the daily rate for a 6' x 6' rack is just high enough to take a lot of profit out of your garage sale. So it's better to borrow. It's even better to build--and it's not as difficult as you think. If you know a plumber who can buy pipe wholesale, have him make one for you.

Planning to have more than one garage sale? Make one yourself. If you're in a neighborhood where some of your friends might go in on the cost, or even the labor, make two or three for everyone to use whenever one wants to have a sale.

OTHER CLOTHES RACKS

Don't be afraid to improvise. Does your house have a front porch? Buy closet pole holders at the hardware store and put up a bar between the posts. Make the bar out of 1-1/8" wood dowelling, cut to the proper length. Support the middle of the bar with wire from above to keep it from sagging under the weight of the clothes.

Steel pipe can be used, but its weight requires sturdier support.

If there's a post or tree next to your garage that you can use, put up a sturdy bar between them. Or use the garage or tree for one end, and a stepladder for the other. Two firmly anchored stepladders with a bar strapped between them will also serve the purpose, but make sure that they can't be knocked over by a passer-by.

A well-supported garage door.

TABLES AS COUNTERS

You'll need tables for displaying items. Card tables, collapsible picnic tables, dinette tables. When you run out of tables and can't borrow more, put boards between tabletops to extend your counter space. Then put planks on top of sawhorses. Since what you're doing is trying to simulate merchandise counters

A PERMANENT CLOTHESRACK
(Can be disassembled for storage)

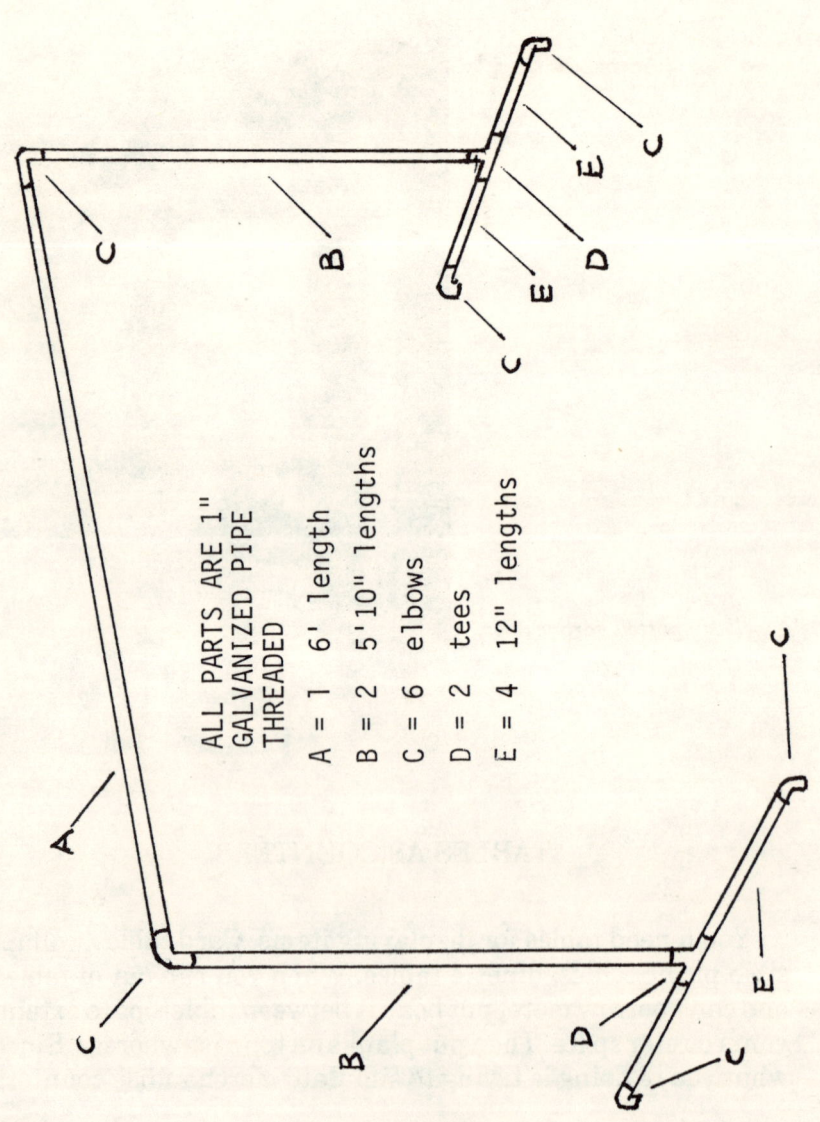

ALL PARTS ARE 1" GALVANIZED PIPE THREADED

A = 1 6' length
B = 2 5'10" lengths
C = 6 elbows
D = 2 tees
E = 4 12" lengths

Be sure to display books in shallow boxes at counter height so that titles can be read. Notice how the hardbound price has been changed.

in a store, you should create as much counterspace as possible.

The objective is to bring the merchandise up closer to the buyer's eyes. Those who arrange small items on blankets spread out on the ground miss this point. Books should be on tables, neatly arranged so the titles can be read easily. A typewriter is awfully hard to try out if it's resting on the grass. Put it at normal operating height, and always have a piece of regular 8-1/2" x 11" typing paper in it.

Toasters, record players, mixers, radios, table lamps, projectors--should not only be on tables, but near an electrical outlet so that they can be plugged in and tested. If something doesn't work, then put it on the ground and mark it as inoperative. If you're lucky, some handyman may buy it.

GROUND LEVEL DISPLAY

The ground is for skis, bowling balls, most auto parts, larger toys and other assorted merchandise...but that doesn't mean these should be simply thrown in a pile! Use a little thought in arranging and displaying what you're selling. The better it's shown off, the faster it will sell.

Anything you can set up and display in its in-use state will sell faster than if it is disassembled, with its parts lying in a pile. If you have the room, put a bed together so the customers can picture it in their own home. Pitch the camper's tent so they'll see that all the parts are there and that it doesn't leak. (A tent on someone's front lawn is a good attention getter for passing traffic.) Not everything belongs in direct sunlight. Record albums will warp (they're best displayed upright, in a box, so they can be leafed-through). Jewelry obviously should be under glass and brought out piece by piece, even costume jewelry, to prevent it "mysteriously walking off." Put it on or near the checkout table where it can be watched.

PRICE EVERYTHING

Sara Smith thinks she's smart. She's having a garage sale, and she deliberately didn't put a price on anything. She's awfully quick-witted, and she plans to improvise and make up the prices orally when someone holds up something and asks about it. She's a clever bargainer, too.

Want to look in and see how smart she really is?

It's ten-thirty in the morning. Sara has made a few sales, which is understandable; she has some good items for sale. Sara doesn't understand, though, why several people who arrived early didn't stay, but took one look, turned and went back to their cars.

But she's doing quite nicely, thank you, answering ques-

This nylon tent proved an excellent way of keeping off the dew, allowing garments to be hung in place the day before the sale. It provided shade on the sunny day that followed.

tions and making change and calling out prices.

More people arrive. This is also understandable, because it's the biggest sales hour of the weekend. And everyone wants to know the price of everything. All at the same time. Too many questions!

"Wally, dear," she calls to her husband, "tell that nice boy how much the camp stove is."

Wally looks at her questioningly. "How much is it?"

Sara is standing at the cashbox with three people in front of her, all holding small items and all waiting to learn the prices. This isn't the way it was supposed to work.

Poor, intelligent Sara doesn't know the half of it. She knows that she's busier than she wants to be, and that the day is going to be an awfully long one. But what she doesn't realize is the number of sales she's losing. Because some people don't like to have to ask prices. They want to see them marked--or they leave. They can't be bothered asking...or they're shy. One woman is about to ask the price of a set of poker chips, but when she hears how much Sara quotes for an ashtray, she puts them back and walks off.

Dissolve to four o'clock in the afternoon. Sara is now quoting lower prices, hoping to get rid of the stuff. Yes, it's selling. But it might have sold early in the morning--at Sara's original price--with the prices marked.

Smart Sara outsmarted herself. She worked harder and made less money.

THE MORAL. Put pricetags on everything. Every book doesn't need one if they're all the same price. But you must print a sign next to them: "Paperbacks 25¢, hardbound 75¢." A row of blouses needs only one sign: "Everything on this rack only 50¢ each!" Or, "Everything on this blanket 10¢ each." Or, "Small items box, your choice 5¢ each." Or, "Old magazines - Take 'em all, 75¢!" The point is, save your own time, but especially your customers' time by letting them know how much it costs them. Or, at least, what the starting price is before the dickering begins. (Haggling, bargaining, etc. is covered at length in Chapter VI).

MARKING PRICES

Nothing is more irritating than to buy something, take it home, and find that the price sticker is almost impossible to remove (try cleaning fluid; it usually works). So be careful where you place stickers, and use the kind that are removable. And never use a felt marker directly on items! Their ink is permanent and there's a chance it may never come off. So the item is ruined.

PLAN YOUR ATTACK

A sale where no one knows what to do is like a chicken coop after a firecracker explodes. You must assign responsibility. Who's going to make change and handle the cashbox? Who's moving the heavy pieces out to the front? Who's supposed to set up tables? Plan it all well in advance, because you won't have the time later.

SECURITY

Thieves, sad to say, are everywhere. They'll not only steal everything not nailed down, they'll steal things that are nailed down--and take the nails, too. Everything at a garage sale is obviously easy pickings.

So be on guard.

"Oh, hi! I was just looking for the kitchen. I wanted to get a glass of water."

This can be more serious than just watching for "Lightfingered Lily," who picks up every one of the tiny porcelain figurines...but doesn't set them all back down. No, it's this serious:

All the family is out in the front yard, working the sale, and someone's upstairs in the bedroom, helping himself or herself to your jewelry. It can't be emphasized enough: Keep the house locked, because in the excitement and distraction of a garage sale, it's very vulnerable.

Then there's the planned caper. Your sale is cased early in the morning, and someone sees something worth "boosting." Later, two cars pull up within minutes of each other. Two people go one way, two another. The first two create a diversion. All of you are distracted. The other pair grab what they want and are in the car and gone with your valuable whatsit in seconds.

SETTING UP

Having a sale in an enclosed backyard has advantages and disadvantages. The disadvantages include a) No display of merchandise out by the street; b) heavy or bulky items must be carried a good distance from the backyard to the street when someone buys them; and c) some people, out of laziness or lack of curiosity, won't bother to walk the extra distance from their cars to your backyard. One disadvantage is easy to solve: simply put the overstuffed chairs, the filing cabinet and the desk in the front yard near the sidewalk. Do plenty of decorating out front, and signs that say "MORE IN THE BACK" to lure them. Also have the prices in plain sight and instructions to pay for the merchandise in back. But for heaven's sake, don't forget about what's out in front! Check on it regularly.

One advantage of the yard sale: security can be tighter in the backyard. You can keep the front door locked and your eye on the back door (if this seems contradictory to the earlier ad-

Two customers are ready to make their purchases and leave--but who's manning the check-out stand? Note the cashbox and adding machine on the card table-and the empty chair.

monition to keep the house locked at all times, it is! But there'll always be someone who wants to go into the house for something, so locking every door can be inconvenient).

Whether it's in front or in back, if you have a long telephone extension or a cordless phone, have it outside so people won't ask to go in the house to make a call. If you're smart, you won't let them use the bathroom or go in for a "drink of water" either.

No matter where you plan to have the sale, there will always be things that you have no intention of selling. Move them as far away from the sale merchandise as you can, or cover them with old sheets to conceal what they are. Mark items that are still prominent with signs that say, "NOT FOR SALE." You'll save yourself endless explaining to people who wish to buy the items.

THE LUXURY OF TIME

But by far the biggest advantage of a backyard sale, assuming that you have an enclosed backyard, is you can begin setting up for the sale days in advance of the big day. Sure, you still have to get up before dawn on Sale Day, but there's none of the mad scrambling to get ready as there is for a sale in your front yard.

The important thing is you can put all your merchandise out the day before-or even earlier--and take your time arranging everything properly. If you leave it uncovered overnight, though, it will be wet with dew (or rain) the next morning. But there's no problem if you buy plastic drop cloths, available at the hardware store. They're cheap, they'll protect it--if they're held firmly in place against the wind--with clothespins or weights.

A FASTER PACE

If your sale is going to be in front of the house, you don't have that luxury of time. So you must hurry on Sale Day. Six o'clock in the morning isn't too early to start (8:00 is the standard opening time). That's without taking time for breakfast. Plan on skipping breakfast. Buy some doughnuts and milk the day before and grab a bite on the run. After all the signs have been put up and everything's in place, someone can make coffee.

GETTING YOUR BUSINESS STRAIGHT

Do you need a permit to have a yard sale in your town? In Southern California it varies from place to place. Call your city hall and ask. You wouldn't want to be closed down in the middle of your sale.

Does everyone in your family know what's being sold? One woman whose husband was out of town sold all of his favorite jackets and sweaters, mistakenly thinking that he didn't want them anymore. They were low-priced and sold fast. And the air was blue in that household for a long time after he returned.

"LET'S HAVE A SALE TOGETHER!"

Those words can be the beginning of a fine sale with a festive atmosphere, or a disorganized mess that strains the bonds of friendship to the limit.

Multi-family sales can be confusing. Two families can usually have a decent sale. But when there's more than two, the problems are compounded. The usual way to identify the merchandise by owner is to mark initials on the pricetags. Color-coding also works, when each family has a different color tag or sticker. Whatever your system, if you plan to split up the money after the sale, you must keep track of what's sold. That

"Of course it works. Just needs a plug."

means a written sales log, recording each transaction.

People from one family won't know the merchandise from another, either. So in addition to the price, mark on a tag or sticker any information that might be helpful. Especially sizes. Collar size and sleeve length on men's shirts. Waist size on pants. Put "it works" on mechanical items that do. Tell whether a cream pitcher is sterling silver or silver plate.

"WHAT IN HECK IS THAT THING?"

They shouldn't have to ask! And you'll save yourself a lot of explanation if you tag those unusual devices.

How an item is identified can often mean the difference in whether it sells or doesn't. Sometimes customers won't recognize a device for what it is, even though it may be something they'd like to own. When it's not mounted on an automobile, a bicycle carrier or a ski rack may not look like anything to someone browsing nearby. You know what it is, but that doesn't mean your customers do. Be sure to describe the use of strange looking items if there's a possibility that some people won't be familiar with them.

"Mark everything!" This was emphasized so strongly at one pre-sale meeting that one or two people took it quite literally. Too literally. On a frying pan was a piece of masking tape that identified it as a "Frying Pan." On a straw hat was another one that said "Straw Hat." Honest!

"If no one comes to your yard sale, your signs are either too few, too small, or too ordinary."

-Geoffery Chaucer

TWO-MAN CHECKOUT TEAMS

It's smart to have two people at the checkout table at a multi-family sale. One can separate the merchandise, by family, that the customer has picked. ("Let's see...this is Martin's can opener and that's Smith's lampshade. And Martin's red blouse, and two books from Powell's" -Along with the prices.) All this information should be recorded on the sales log by the cashier if possible. It can just be a yellow pad, listing items and amounts, under each family's own column. Or each family can have a separate page--although this requires a lot of flipping back and forth.

After the customer's items are sorted by family and recorded (item and price), the cashier adds the figures (You DO have an adding machine or a calculator, don't you?); takes the money and makes change from the cashbox. Only one person should handle the cash at a time. If you don't have a cashbox, a fishing tackle box can work, but be careful of leaving the metal box in the hot sun for very long. Also, Tupperware makes a fine plastic box which we assume is for buttons, thread, etc. It has compartments that serve for bills and coins, and a lid that keeps wind, rain and idle hands out of the money. Some people wear carpenter's aprons--but for multi-family sales, you'll be hopelessly confused at accounting time.

Despite how careful you are about logging each sale by family, unless there's a professional bookkeeper among you, it will be a miracle if the books balance at the end of the day. Consider yourselves lucky if you come within a few dollars of being able to give each family its proper share.

Church and other charity rummage sales require a lot more planning and organization than we've mentioned here. And there's usually someone in the organization who knows the procedures. If you are part of a club that has never had a sale and wants to, just remember: a) delegate responsibility; b) plan well in advance; c) have enough volunteer help; d) stay security-minded...even if your customers are all sweet old ladies who look like they wouldn't even take an extra sugar cube in a restaurant. Don't count on it. You haven't seen deep down in their purses.

DON'T FORGET CHANGE

It's such a simple thing to remember. The people who are getting ready to have a garage sale are going to be dealing with money. Yet they so often forget to have enough change on hand when they open up. There's no standard rule that we know of, but it's good to have at least 20 one dollar bills, a half dozen fives, a few tens, and about five dollars in silver. Unless you're planning to do some cutesy pricing like $1.98, forget pennies. Round off your prices and spare yourself a big headache.

The important thing is: don't forget change!

LAST...BUT FOREMOST: SAFETY!

In holding a garage or yard sale, you are in effect inviting people onto your property. And under the law, in doing so, you become to a large degree responsible for their safety. Therefore you should make every effort to see that accidents don't occur. For two very major reasons: You certainly don't want anyone to be injured. And if someone were injured on your property and you were to be found negligent in a court of law--you'd stand to lose not merely a considerable sum of money, but possibly your home and anything else you own.

That's why it pays to remove any potential causes of accidents before your sale--and post highly visible warnings of any hazards that you cannot remove.

Long before you open for business, pretend you're a stranger. Walk around your property and look for those things that you're so familiar with and take for granted--but might pose a problem to a first-time visitor. Is there a flagstone walk or some other walkway with unsure footing? Is there a bush which must be pushed aside so one can proceed--which then snaps back--that could possibly hurt someone? Is there a steep incline; are there uneven steps; a narrow passage? Obviously you don't post a sign that warns of an unlighted passageway, you light it.

A simple sign with an arrow saying, "Watch your step!" may save you untold thousands of dollars in a court case.

Don't position a tall breakfront on the edge of a driveway where it might possibly be tipped over on a passing child. Make sure that your clothesracks are strong and solid; that your garage door won't come down accidentally; that there's no puddle or oil slick to slip on. And route everybody away from your swimming pool.

Have each member of your garage sale crew spend some time looking for safety hazards long before your sale starts. Make sure that if anything does happen, it won't be your fault!

THE 5 MOST COMMON GARAGE SALE MISTAKES

(Which are you guilty of?)

1 DISPLAY — Merchandise not clean; in poor condition; or left in boxes that the customer is expected to dig through

2 PRICES — Too high; unrealistic; too firm (the owner is not prepared to dicker)

3 CHANGE — No silver or small bills on hand to make change for customers

4 SIGNS — Not enough of them; they're too small; the lettering is too thin; hard to read even from a stopped car

5 PREPARATION — Not ready at announced opening time; merchandise not priced; owner still undecided on prices

Chapter V

THE SALE

There are times to be serious at garage sales and other times to lighten up and relax.

Since the biggest sales hours of the entire weekend are from nine to eleven on Saturday morning, it doesn't pay to blow it by starting on the bloody marys at eight. It's best to save the partying until later in the day--when the customer traffic has lessened, the tension and excitement are over, and most of the day's sales have been made.

So it's the morning of the sale, and we're serious. Let's get everybody up early to help. At least by six. Put those signs up all over the neighborhood. If they're all lettered and ready to erect; and if you know all the places to put them, it shouldn't take a whole hour--if you hustle. So the sign crew should be back before seven--to help in setting up.

If you're lucky and have good friends to help, they'll be there early, too, cheerful and ready to work. If you're really lucky, perhaps one of them will have brought a cake she'd baked the night before.

Set up the card tables and start arranging the merchandise. Leave the heavier items for the male members of the family to move. Work fast and have little wasted effort, because you'll need every bit of the time available to get ready for the buyers, who, by the way, will probably be there before you want them.

Park the family cars down the street, at least two doors down from your house, so that customers have easy access to the sale area. See if a neighbor can't be persuaded to keep your family dog in his or her backyard. Even if your mutt is a friendly one, not everyone likes dogs, and the objective is to make the garage sale as inviting to as many customers as possible.

Check to see that every item for sale has a price on it, except for garments and books, which are sorted in clothesracks and boxes (shallow) and clearly marked. Earlier in the week, you and one or two friends should have spent the best part of a day sorting and pricing the clothes. Now each blouse, skirt and dress has an identifying mark of some sort. The best way to mark them seems to be a piece of paper and an old fashioned straight pin. Colored stickers fall off after a day or two. Staples can tear fabrics when they're being removed.

Have paper bags and plastic shopping bags on hand to put merchandise in when purchased--as well as newspaper to wrap around breakables.

THE ALL-IMPORTANT CASHBOX

The cashbox has enough cash in it to make change for a twenty dollar bill. Whoever is assigned to man it should know the merchandise and most of the prices without looking at the pricetags--at least at the start. Later, when others have become familiar with the merchandise, they can take over.

Everyone must be aware of the importance of guarding the cashbox well. It should never be out of the cashier's line of vision. The cashbox is the most important item at any garage sale, and during the course of the day, it should be emptied of any accumulation of big bills. Take them inside the house for safekeeping. The house remains locked, if at all possible.

OPENING UP

Chances are, if you've done a good job of promoting your sale, you'll have people there, waiting for you to open up. Fine. If it's 7:48 and you're due to open at 8:00, they'll usually wait patiently until the hour. If it's 8:15 and you were supposed to open at 8:00, try to accommodate them as best you can while you're setting up. Don't be like some people we've seen, who, for no other reason than they can't get their act together, become all snotty and officious and say, "We're not open yet. You'll just have to wait--or come back later." What wonderful sales technique.

KIDS

Kids are special and we all love'em, but the truth is, they don't belong at garage sales. Before you mention how many toys are sold at garage sales, remember that toy store owners aren't too crazy about having kids running around in their stores, playing with all the merchandise, either.

If possible, keep your own kids out of the way. When your children are a bit older, they can help, of course--and even be enlisted to help keep the neighborhood kids from hanging around your sale--which after all, is a local event. Don't let them disturb your customers.

Kids rarely make good sales people, so don't go away and leave them in charge. They can be intimidated by adult customers and make serious mistakes.

Great idea! Make a kiosk with your prices on all four sides by using a big carton placed atop an empty garbage can.

OTHER POINTS

If a customer buys something big, he or she may pay for it and plan to come back with a station wagon or a truck. Be sure to mark the item "sold." It helps if you add the person's name, too.

At one garage sale we held, a lady liked a chair on display. It was worth about twenty-five dollars; we had it priced at fifteen. She bargained for it and got us to reduce the price to five.

She paid cash, her name was put on it under the word "sold," and she promised to come back in a few hours with her husband to collect it.

She never returned. The chair sat on our back porch, with her name on it, for a month. We've had many theories about why she never came back. One is that she found our house by following the signs. When the signs were taken down, she didn't know where we lived--and where her new chair was!

TAKING DEPOSITS

It's important to establish a strict policy on taking deposits. Some sellers are against taking them, saying that they've had too many people come back and say they've changed their minds and ask for their deposits back. This has been costly to the seller, who may have had other chances to sell the item-- and while it was still early enough to sell at maximum price.

Others have made it clear that all deposits are non-refundable, and they make a point of writing that on the receipt. Many people will balk at this, but it's one way of ensuring that the sellers are compensated for their inconvenience.

Still others will take a deposit on something, say ten dollars on a forty dollar item, and tell the customer that they'll hold it in his or her name for an hour or two at the most.

Evidence of a well-advertised garage sale. There is not a parking space to be had within a block at 10 a.m. on this Saturday morning.

DON'T BE STAMPEDED

A tactic used by some buyers often works to send the cashier into a state of confusion--with the result that merchandise is sold too cheaply. A customer will bring a dozen or so different items to the checkout table, act very busy and in a hurry, and say, "How much for the whole bunch?" Or, "Here's all this stuff. Will you take six dollars for the whole lot?"

One man we know who specializes in buying tools will look over the whole tool display, then say, "I'll give you ten dollars for all of "em." Since it's usually early in the day, and since tools are a high-demand item, the seller stands to lose a considerable amount of profit. The offer is always tempting; after all, it's an opportunity to clear out lots of merchandise with one quick sale.

Be fair to yourself and to the sale you've worked hard to organize. Don't be stampeded. Take your time and consider. Use your adding machine and learn the total that the items would bring if sold individually as planned. If the offer comes within ten or fifteen percent of the total (which is unlikely), you may be better off accepting it. The more likely case is that you stand to lose--so simply say, "No, thanks, it's too early in the day for that. They're for sale individually--priced as marked."

Chances are, there'll be no scene, no temper outburst. The people who shop that way are old hands at it and are used to being rebuffed. They'll shrug and move on...because time is important to them. As they leave, it doesn't hurt to say, "Why don't you come back about four o'clock? Maybe we can do business then."

Enclosed yards make it possible to set up well in advance. If you plan your sale for more than one day, repositioning the tables after the first day will save your lawn from damage from heavy foot traffic.

SHOULD YOU TAKE CHECKS?

Anyone with a checkbook is assumed to have financial responsibility. But you shouldn't assume it, even if you decide to accept personal checks.

There are two schools of thought about checks. One is a firm policy of not accepting them--and a sign backing it up that says, "NO CHECKS." The reasoning is, if someone does have a checkbook and plenty of identification, there's no reason why that person can't go to a nearby supermarket and get the cash to pay for your merchandise. And if they want the item badly enough, they'll do it.

The other policy holds that if you're in business to sell merchandise, you must be accommodating to your customers. If the sale is more than $5.00, take a check. Ask for a driver's license for identification. Make sure the address is a local one and that it matches the one on the check. If you really want to avoid being stung, record the license number, the birthdate of the person, and the expiration date of the license.

It may seem surprising, but garage sale veterans say that they've been burned less by bad checks than they have by sticky-fingered shoppers. This may be because in some states it's a felony to write a check deliberately on an account that has insufficient funds.

SO MUCH FOR FAME

Two friends of ours who handle estate sales on a percentage basis were finishing up a long-running estate sale in the San Fernando Valley section of Los Angeles. They were taking checks, but required identification that included a driver's license and a credit card. Two young men dressed in scruffy jeans and flannel shirts were looking over a selection of rings, and one of them decided to buy two rings with turquoise stones. He wrote out a check, but when asked for I.D., said he didn't have any with him.

"Sorry," the one woman said, "without I.D., we can't take your check."

Smiling, the man said, "Lady, I'm Joe Montana." The

woman brightened immediately. "Oh, are you related to Monty Montana, who rides the horse in the Rose Bowl Parade every year?"

The buyer, whose friend began laughing hysterically, said, "No, ma'm, I'm Joe Montana. I play football."

The woman looked at her friend, who admitted ignorance with a shrug, then turned back to Joe Montana. "Well, I don't care who you are, we can't take your check without I.D."

Joe Montana went home, got his driver's license and returned to buy the rings. A few Sundays later as she was passing through the living room, she was to remember the incident when her husband mentioned that her ring customer had just thrown a touchdown pass for the San Francisco Forty Niners.

"Sorry it doesn't have a price tag. But how can I price it when I don't know what it is?"

NEATEST TRICK OF THE WEEK

Ever hear of anyone selling something twice at the same garage sale? -With all parties concerned thoroughly satisfied?

It happened at a one-day charity yard sale held for theSanta Ana Emblem Club #530, a woman's charitable organization made up of Elks' wives. A member had donated six twin beds which had been in furnished bachelor apartments of her apartment complex.

Like most furniture that is still clean and serviceable, it was about to be snapped up quickly at the sale. In fact, there were several people vying for the right to buy them, each arguing about who had been there first and had the legitimate claim.

The Emblem Club cashier was firm. "I'm sorry," she said, "but this lady was first, and she wants all of them." Groans could be heard from others who wanted one or two of the beds.

"You know, it's a shame," said the lady customer. "The fact is, I need the beds for only one week. I'm going to be entertaining a group of teenage students, and when they're gone, I don't know what I'll do with the beds." She explained that she'd originally planned on renting beds, but when she learned that the rental store wanted $30 each for the week, she decided to try her luck at garage sales. The Club's beds were $10 each.

"That's no problem," said the enterprising Emblem Club cashier. "Just give these other people who want the beds your name and address, and they can come to your house and buy the beds from you next week when the students leave." There was quick agreement all around.

Remarkable what a bit of communication can do to make everyone happy.

KEEP IT MOVING

Be alert to why an item doesn't sell. Is it too highpriced? Is it something that the customers can't figure out, and it must be explained? Before you lower the price, print a sign that explains what the thing does. That may be all it takes.

People love anything that is half-price. Some sellers have a half-price table, where they place things that they really never want to see again, such as puka shell necklaces and monkey pod dishes. As the day wears on, more and more items hit the half-price table.

When sales have slowed to a crawl, it's time to give them a boost with a "half-price sale" on everything! Dresses that didn't sell for a dollar are suddenly snatched up. Books that a buyer was only mildly interested in a moment ago become so cheap that it's silly not to take all of them.

When it's half-price time, don't forget your signs! Send your younger helpers out to staple or tape "EVERYTHING HALF PRICE!" on the signs leading to your sale.

STUFF A BAG FOR A BUCK

When it's late in the day and activity is winding down, a great way to stimulate business is to offer large grocery bags--either paper or plastic--for a dollar...and let them fill the bags with anything they wish. This is especially good if you plan to have everything left at your sale picked up by a charity organization. Have your signmaker-in-residence make a quick one that says in big letters, "Anything you can fit in a bag--only $1.00!" Then have one of the workers (the one with the most energy remaining) hold it up to passing motorists.

The thought of the bargains to be had for such a small investment is irresistible. We've seen 40 or 50 bags sold for a dollar each in the space of a half hour late in the afternoon.

On a large front lawn with much merchandise to display, drive stakes into the ground and stretch string across the front to create a "Main Entrance." Note box-sign stapled to top of one of the stakes. Also that the big items like furniture are placed near the street.

EXPLAIN THIS ONE

A man walked up to a check-out table holding a beer can opener which had no price on it. (He'd taken it off a table marked "ALL ITEMS 5c.") How much is this? he asked. The woman looked at it. "I think that's five cents," she answered.

The man examined it for a moment, deep in thought, then returned to the five cent table, put it back, and left.

YOU SHOULD KNOW BETTER!

When you're having a Saturday-Sunday sale and you find that you still have more than fifty percent of your merchandise left on Sunday morning, your prices are too high.

This means that you must either cut your prices at once, or be prepared to put all your junk back into the basement and attic.

Be serious! If you really think that someone is going to pay $75 for your nine-year-old stereo console, you don't understand the reality of garage sales. It doesn't matter that it's solid oak, works perfectly, and that you bought it for $900. In today's market, with incredible advances in electronics technology almost daily, the demand for your stereo is minimal.

You may be better off, if there's some sentimental attachment to the stereo, giving it to someone you know.

Chapter VI

YOU BE THE CUSTOMER

Is it worth it? Can one really find bargains among other people's junk? If you're not a diehard collector of china, antiques or first editions, why should visiting garage sales interest you?

It's true: most people go to garage sales more for fun than for profit. But sometimes the funseekers come away with a lot more than they expected. We know personally of a woman who found a 25-ft. fiberglass sailing sloop, in excellent condition, on its own trailer, priced at $2500. She wrote out a check and paid for it on the spot, then called her husband. With his own trailer hitch, he towed it away less than an hour later. A week later, the former owners, who'd been so hasty in their need for money, came to return the $2500 and reclaim the boat. But the happy buyers weren't home; they were out sailing.

Another woman bought a Hummel figurine at a garage sale

for three dollars. Simply because she liked it. It was later appraised, at a friend's urging, for over a thousand dollars.

There are many stories to match these. In most cases, however, the person did a lot of looking before making that one incredible "find."

HOW'S YOUR ATTITUDE?

To be successful at garage saling, some lifelong feelings you've had may have to be set aside. One may be a hesitancy to buy second hand merchandise. It probably has something to do with the way you were brought up. You feel that using something that once belonged to a total stranger is, if not actually wrong, well, rather tacky. Used cars and boats may be all right, of course. Antiques, too, silly. But anything else? Yuck!

What a pity. Your attitude may keep you from some highly advantageous purchases. It's one only the very rich can afford. (Even millionaires have been known to buy something they want at a bargain price, used or not.) Another thing to remember is that not everything on sale at a garage sale is used. People often sell new, sealed, clean, unworn or unused merchandise at garage sales for remarkably low prices.

Let's go a step further. How do you feel about buying things that belonged to someone who's recently died? Would that bother you? Make you feel a bit ghoulish? We say forget it. Especially because some of your best buys are to be had at estate sales, which are often held to liquidate the belongings of someone deceased. And what real difference is there if the former owner is living or dead? If it's something you can use, buy it!

GARAGE SALE TALES

HOW ABOUT CLOTHES?

Garments that have been worn before may present a problem. Whether that problem is a major or minor one will depend on whether you had any brothers or sisters who borrowed from each other...or even if you lived in a dormitory where wearing other people's clothes was limited only by who got them first and whether or not they fit (many times they're borrowed when they don't fit at all).

At any rate, as long as you wash or dryclean the garments you buy before you wear them there's no problem--unless you insist on creating one in your own mind.

GETTING STARTED

It is a Wednesday afternoon in Orange, California. Although the first of the weekend garage sales is still two days away, Betty Wilson sits at her kitchen table, reading the Pennysaver which arrived in the noon mail. She has a yellow pad, a magnifying glass, and a Thomas Bros. map book of Orange County cities next to her.

The Pennysaver contains page after page of unclassified ads. As she turns the pages, her sharp eye quickly separates the ads for garage sales from those for used cars, tree-trimming services, guitar lessons and lost dogs.

MOVING SALE. G.E. upright freezer, 15 cu. ft., mattress & box spring, solid oak coffee table, Singer sewing machine (6 yrs.), working color TV, lamps, pictures. 12373 Addaway (Farmer/Glassell), Sat. only 8-5.

Betty turns to the second sheet of her yellow pad, marked "Saturday" at the top. She adds the basic facts from the ad to her list: "12373 Addaway (Farmer/Glassell) 8 am." If she's not familiar with Addaway Street, she'll search it out on one of the pages in the map book, then add simple directions to her previous notation. Later she'll map out her route so that she and Ethel, her garage sale partner in crime, will be able to hop from one sale to another with a minimum of backtracking.

As she reads the ads and jots down the addresses, she has a pretty good idea whether a sale is going to be worthwhile or not. The neighborhood usually tells. The best garage sales seem to be found in pride-of-ownership areas with medium-priced homes. For many, it's interim housing; they're moving up the economic ladder and leaving their first homes. And the junk they've accumulated in the past ten years isn't going with them. The prices are usually good because they really don't care about keeping anything.

Rundown neighborhoods seldom have what Betty wants. Not that she won't jot down the address of the sale and be there on the weekend; she just knows better than to have her hopes high. It will be mostly junk; broken toys, some old tires and an auto horn. Once in a while there'll be a gem...and it will justify the visit.

Rich neighborhoods are strange. The prices are often unrealistic. A dress that cost $349 originally is still a used dress at a garage sale. But often its owner can't face the indignity of dropping the price to the going garage-sale level.

Betty knows better than to pass up a sale at a fancy home, however. There's always the chance of finding an expensive piece of furniture in remarkable condition for a fraction of what it cost. When that happens, Betty's weekend has been made; her life fulfilled. Betty continues working. The Friday sales are listed on the first yellow sheet; the Sunday-onlys on the third. Once in a while there's a garage sale that starts on a Thursday. She'll make a special note of it and be sure to alert Ethel. They'll be there. The early shoppers get the good bargains.

A NEW ADVENTURE EVERY WEEKEND

Betty and Ethel are two of the millions who have made garage saling an avocation, done week in and week out, even on holiday weekends--although few are usually scheduled then.

If you were to ask them, they'd freely admit that their main reason for garage saling is not to find the Buy of the Century--although they're looking for it in dead seriousness--it's because they're having so much fun. As in many sports, the ones who take them seriously and spend the most time in preparation for the sport are usually the ones who derive the most enjoyment from it.

Like Betty and Ethel, two-women teams are on the go--not just on Saturday mornings, but most of the week--communicating, preparing, exploring. Each woman may have a specialty. One may like rattan furniture or rare books; the other fine china or stuffed animals. They keep their eyes open for their partner's needs as well as their own.

Like Betty, they map out their routes. They know that a couple can hit only so many garage sales in a day, so they learn what areas are best and concentrate on them...visiting the others only after the good sales are exhausted.

THE BIG DAY

Betty's up at six on Saturday because it's important to get started early. She puts on an outfit that will make it easy for her to try on clothes. She wears a short sleeved or sleeveless blouse under a sweater which she can remove if the day becomes too warm or so she can try on different tops to see how they fit. She also wears slacks, and knee-highs, not socks, to try on shoes.

When Betty leaves the house, she has the yellow pad with the route mapped out, a purse with many dollar bills and quarters (because many people having sales forget a simple thing like having change), and a list of items she's looking for. Some of the items are things that other people want. Her sister wants a night table for her bedroom. Betty has the dimensions of the space it's to fit. Other people, knowing she can spot such things, have asked her to look for carved chessmen; any books on Hollywood or old movies; wicker lamps; and musical instruments. She also has a tape measure with which she can measure rugs, pants, and the night table, if she finds one.

NEGOTIATING: MY PRICE OR YOURS?

A Southern California driveway will never resemble a Middle Eastern bazaar. You won't hear a Santa Ana housewife, if offered too low a price for her armoire, wail that her ancestors are being insulted. But her ""precious heirloom" may have been in the family all of three weeks--having been purchased at a garage sale in Garden Grove. Yes, the dialogue may differ, but the attitudes are similar...and it's always *caveat emptor*--let the buyer beware.

Haggling, hondeling, chiseling, dickering, bargaining...there are many names for it. But they all concern a buyer and a seller arguing about the price to be paid for an item.

Some haven't the nerve to argue. With other people, those who've paid the asking price for everything all their lives, the idea of negotiating never crosses their minds. Still others, after immersing themselves in the Saturday garage sale scene long enough, know that it's part of the fun.

Indeed, persuading a seller to settle for less than his or her original price can become an obsession. Some consider paying "list price" for anything a cardinal sin in the first place. So they love garage sales. To them, the figure on a pricetag is there to be lowered. Their mission is to make the owner part with the item for less...and the compulsion to "beat him down" may even overpower the desire for the item itself.

In Betty's case, haggling isn't a compulsion--but it's fun.

Learning to bargain wasn't hard. Once she'd summoned the courage to offer less than the marked price at one garage sale, it became increasingly easier. Betty also remembered a favorite quotation of her father's: *Audentes fortuna juvat;* "Fortune favors the bold." On this Saturday morning, Betty sees a table lamp. She likes it, she knows just where it will go in her home. The seller has plainly marked it at $15. But why should Betty pay $15 for it when she may be able to get it cheaper?

She starts her attack by engaging the seller in conversation. Break the ice. Talking about the weather is trite, and it really doesn't disarm anyone. Betty tries something else. She looks for some way to warm up the woman, a middle-aged lady Betty hasn't seen before. She's never had a garage sale before, as Betty remembers. She tries to find something nice to say about her house. her flower garden, the car in the driveway, the way the merchandise is arranged.

If there's a dog or cat in view, Betty, a true animal lover, will make friends with it, as only some people can. This is a tried and true disarming tactic. But there's no animal in sight.

Betty remembers the signs leading to the sale. They were adequate. Betty tells the lady they were great. A slight smile of thanks. It's working.

After she looks at the lamp, Betty moves away from it. She doesn't intend for the seller to know she wants it...or could possible be serious about buying it. That's a trap many people fall into in automobile showrooms and used car lots: once the salesman sees you're interested in a particular car, you're dead meat.

Looking at something else, Betty continues the conversation. Then, when she's six or eight feet away from it, she points back at the lamp and says, "By the way, what are you asking for that table lamp over there?" Casually.

Since she's not standing right in front of it and looking at the pricetag, there's nothing offensive or insulting in her question.

How the woman answers will determine what follows. Betty listens carefully to the lady's inflection, and watches her body language. If the woman's tone is firm, her stance strong, Betty may enlist the help of Ethel, who is across the way, looking at lace tablecloths.

"Ethel, isn't that lamp like the one we saw at that other house?"

Ethel's quick on the uptake. "Identical. And they wanted five dollars for that one, as I remember."

Such a ploy isn't necessary in this case. When asked the price, the woman's remark is casual. "Oh, fifteen dollars, I guess."

The answer is accompanied by a slight shrug. Inwardly, Betty is jubilant. The woman is ready for the slaughter. Or-

"When do you think you'll be back for the dining room set?"

dinarily, Betty would start at half the asking price. In this case, she dares to offer less than half. She may not get it, but it's definitely worth the try. Because the owner "told" her with her body language and the tone of her voice that she isn't on firm ground.

"Would you take five dollars for it?" Betty brazenly asks--but in the gentlest, friendliest, pleasantest tone she can summon.

Not much later, Ethel helps Betty load the lamp in the back of her station wagon after paying eight dollars for it.

THE BUD VASE

At the opposite end of the spectrum is the person whose bargaining methods are so offensive that he or she is obnoxious to everyone. The manners of such people are so irritating that they are successful with only the most timid sellers.

At a charity sale given by a church one weekend, a woman took a fancy to a bud vase that was clearly marked seventy-five cents. She carried it to the two women sitting at the cashier's table.

"You take a quarter for this?" She asked them.

"Gee, no," the one said, "We didn't do the pricing, and I don't know if we're allowed to..."

"You won't take a quarter for it?" The customer repeated.

The other cashier spoke. "Sorry. It's seventy-five cents."

The woman returned the bud vase to its table and continued looking at the merchandise. A few minutes later, she came back to the table with the same vase.

"Now will you take a quarter for it?"

The two cashiers looked at each other. They nodded, then one smiled and spoke. "You can have it for fifty cents."

"I'll give you a quarter for it."

"No, really. It's a nice vase, and fifty cents is a fair price."

Again the woman put the bud vase back and moved on.

The same scene, played with almost identical dialogue, took place a few minutes later. The mood at the check-out table had changed. The two young women had been so put off by the woman's humorless, demanding manner that working the sale wasn't fun anymore. If the woman had been at all nice, the vase would have been hers at whatever price. But they again refused the twenty-five cents, and the woman, now irate, set the vase down forcefully on the card table, stalked to her car, and drove off.

Toward the end of the afternoon, the woman reappeared. She saw the bud vase on the table.

"Good! It's still here." A glint appeared in the corner of her eye. "NOW you will take a quarter for it!" She was ready to claim her prize and leave in triumph. One of the young women stood up, and, picking up the vase, dropped it on the sidewalk. It broke into a dozen pieces. "NOW you can have it for a quarter," she said calmly, while returning the woman's stare.

As the obnoxious customer made her way to her car, the one who had broken the vase took seventy-five cents out of her purse and put the money in the church's cashbox.

WHAT DO YOU SAY?

Sparring doesn't come easily to some people. If you're one of them, it may pay you to learn a couple of phrases which may save money for you in garage sale transactions. Rephrase them as you wish, but keep the thought:

"I don't know, it really isn't what I want, but--well, would you take $_____ for it?"

"You're asking $_____? Oh, golly, thats more than I was thinking of paying. Could you come down a bit?"

"I really hadn't planned on paying that much. Don't you

think $_____ would be a better price?"

None of these is particularly overwhelming or guaranteed to devastate your opponent, but each can help to open the gates to negotiation, and sometimes that's enough to bring you a lower price.

Crystal and glassware gleaming temptingly in the morning sun. There's a good chance that most of it was gone by afternoon.

CAVEAT EMPTOR?

Unless you're a licensed mechanic, an electronics expert, or one heckuva handyman, it's easy to make a mistake in buying mechanical, electronic or electrical equipment at a garage sale. It doesn't have to be a personal computer. The item may be as unsophisticated as a toaster or an iron. But if you take someone's word for the fact that it works--it may cost you. The seller's counting on finding a gullible customer like you.

Many times you'll hear that a child's electrical toy "Just needs batteries." Sure it does. The TV set works fine, but there's no place to plug it in. Don't buy it until it is plugged in--and has a good picture on every channel (it can have a great one on a single channel but the tuner can be broken).

"The guy who owns it could tell you all about it, but he isn't here right now," is an often heard phrase. You shouldn't be there, either.

If by chance the owner is there, don't be afraid to ask to turn it on, ask how it works, ask why he's getting rid of it. The important thing is to make sure it's in good working condition. You're inviting trouble if you think that, once you've bought it at a cheap price, you can spend a few bucks to have it repaired, and everything will be wonderful.

But ask yourself: If it took only "a few bucks" to put it in operating condition, why doesn't the owner make that investment himself?

"Whenever you buy or sell . . . make a definite bargain, and never trust to the flattering lie, 'We shan't disagree about trifles.'"

-George Macdonald

BY THE WAY

We came by much of this knowledge the hard way. One Sunday at a swap meet in Miami, we saw a shiny, name-brand chrome toaster on display for only five dollars. The nicest little old lady was selling it in her rented space, along with many miscellaneous items.

"Does it work?" we asked, wondering about the low price.

"Of course. It works perfectly," she said with a reassuring tone while smiling sweetly. "I'm sorry there isn't any place around here to plug it in."

We bought it. It didn't work.

The authors.

THE 6 WORST CUSTOMER FAULTS

UNPREPAREDNESS — Carrying only big bills; not having ready cash to snap up something that will sell quickly. Not dressing properly so you can try on garments.

OPTIMISM — Assuming perfection. If you buy something before first seeing that it works, you're the sucker they were waiting for.

LACK OF VISION — Failing to see a diamond in the rough; passing over tarnished or reparable articles that could be worth many times the asking price.

GULLIBILITY — Believing everything you hear. If you really think that a little bracelet belonged to the Queen of Thailand, we have some choice swampland to sell you.

TIMIDITY — Being afraid to bargain. Remember, it never hurts to try - and the money you save may be your own.

LETHARGY — Not getting out early enough. Not moving fast enough; wasting time at a mediocre sale instead of moving on. The more you visit, the more chances to find real bargains.

Chapter VII

FIRMLY COMMITTED?
OR REALLY INDIFFERENT?

You've probably known people who, when they take up a sport, really "take up a sport." They invest in the best equipment they can afford (sometimes it's equipment they can't afford); they buy the latest outfits in which to play the game; they pay for lessons. From then on, it's intense practice, competition only with those who play better than they do, and a win-at-all-costs attitude that grows stronger as their involvement becomes total.

That's serious.

There are others who'll grab any old piece of equipment and play the same game with spirit, enjoying every minute of it--whether they win or lose. After all, it's for fun, right?

Who's right?

A garage sale can be a great little party if you like. What's more pleasant on a Saturday afternoon than two or three couples, all close friends, sitting out on the lawn on folding chairs, basking in the sun? The music's playing, and those who haven't cans of beer in their hands have coffee mugs. With bloody marys or daiquiris in them.

And if someone wants to buy any of the merchandise on display, fine. The casual approach to garage saling.

The direct opposite: the serious folks. Their pleasure comes from looking at the bottom line and finding satisfactory profit.

Thus we find that, as in any endeavor, there are different levels of commitment. Most people will opt for a moderate course somewhere in between these two examples...mixing a bit of fun with enough seriousness to get rid of their castoffs (the original objective) and making some extra money, too.

Whichever course you choose, we strongly believe that you'll be most successful if you follow the suggestions in this book. Study other sales to guide you in pricing your items. Use price tags. Delegate responsibility. Plan your security. Advertise in your local shopper. Put up compelling signs, the bigger the better. Open on time. Have enough change on hand. Watch your cashbox. Don't be afraid to haggle--but don't be beaten down below your rock bottom price. And have fun.

See you next Saturday morning!

THE END

Photos taken in the authors' home. With a few exceptions like the dining room chandelier and original paintings, everything was bought at a garage sale -- at a price far below its true value.

WOULD AUNT SOPHIE LIKE THIS BOOK?

Know any garage sale fanatics? Or anyone who really needs help -because they have such terrible garage sales? "Trash and Treasure" makes a great gift! Order the extras copies you want now at these terrific discount prices!

1 book	$7.95
2 - 4 books	$6.35 ea.
5 - 9 books	$5.95 ea.
10 - 24 books	$5.55 ea.
25 or more books	$4.35 ea.

(Calif. residents add 6% sales tax.)
Shipping: $1 for the first book and 50¢ for each additional book

(In a hurry? Add $3 per book for air mail)

ORDER FORM

Bent Twig Publishing Co.
1088 Irvine, Blvd., Suite 329
Tustin, California 92680

Please send me _____ copies of "Trash and Treasure." I enclose my check or money order for $_____ (include shipping charge and Calif. sales tax, if applicable)

Name _____

Address _____

City _____ State ___ Zip _____

(COPY THIS FORM IF YOU WANT TO KEEP THE BOOK INTACT)